NJINGA
OF NDONGO AND MATAMBA
COLORING AND ACTIVITY BOOK

Copyright © 2021 Our Ancestories

All rights reserved. No part of this publication may be reproduced, distributed, or transmitted in any form or by any means, including photocopying, recording, or other electronic or mechanical methods, without the prior written permission of the publisher, except in the case of brief quotations embodied in critical reviews and certain other noncommercial uses permitted by copyright law.

ISBN: 978-1-7771179-6-2 (Paperback)

First Print Edition

www.our-ancestories.com

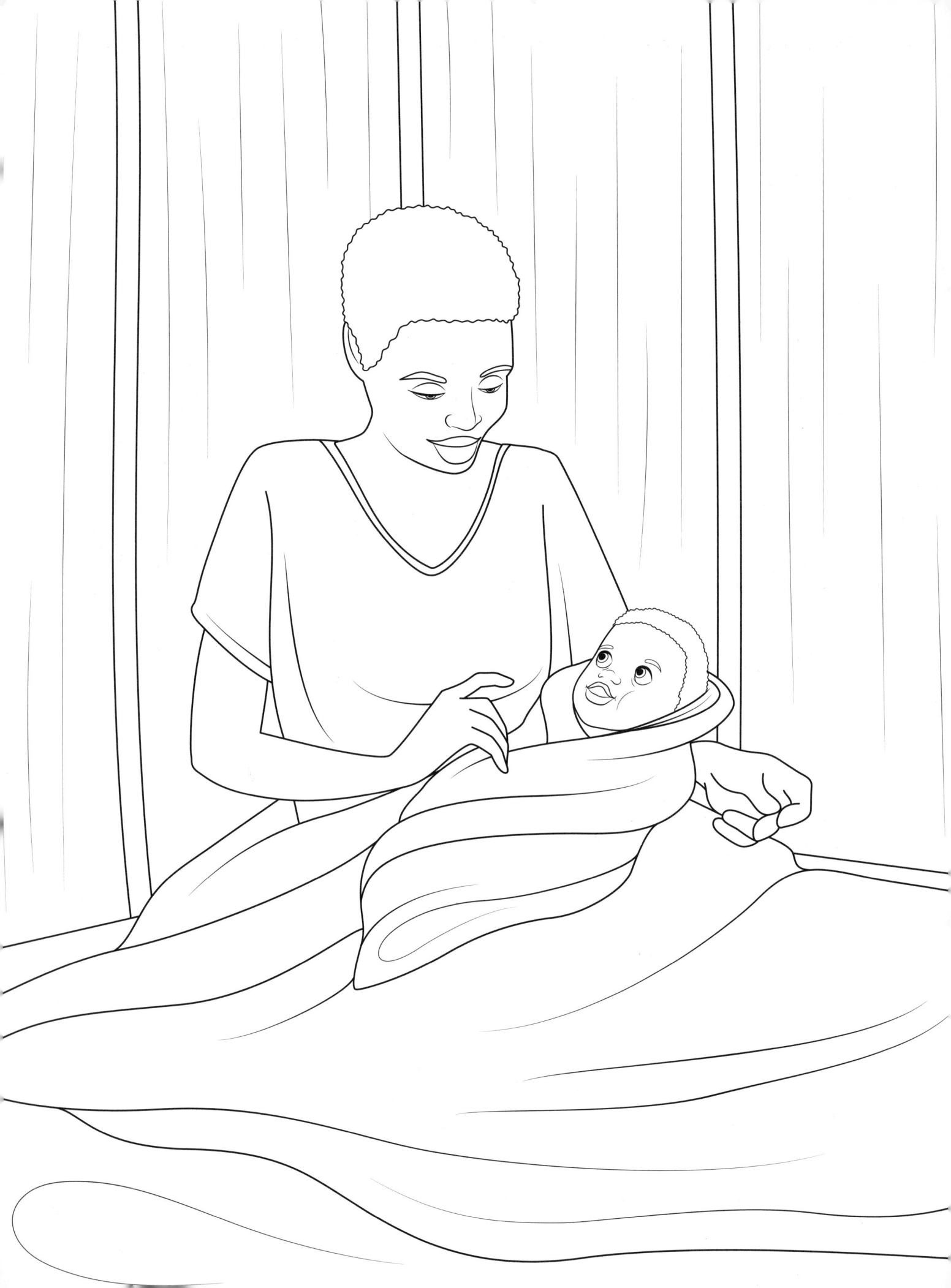

Njinga Goes to School

A Maze. Help Njinga find her way to school so she can learn! Trace the path through the maze.

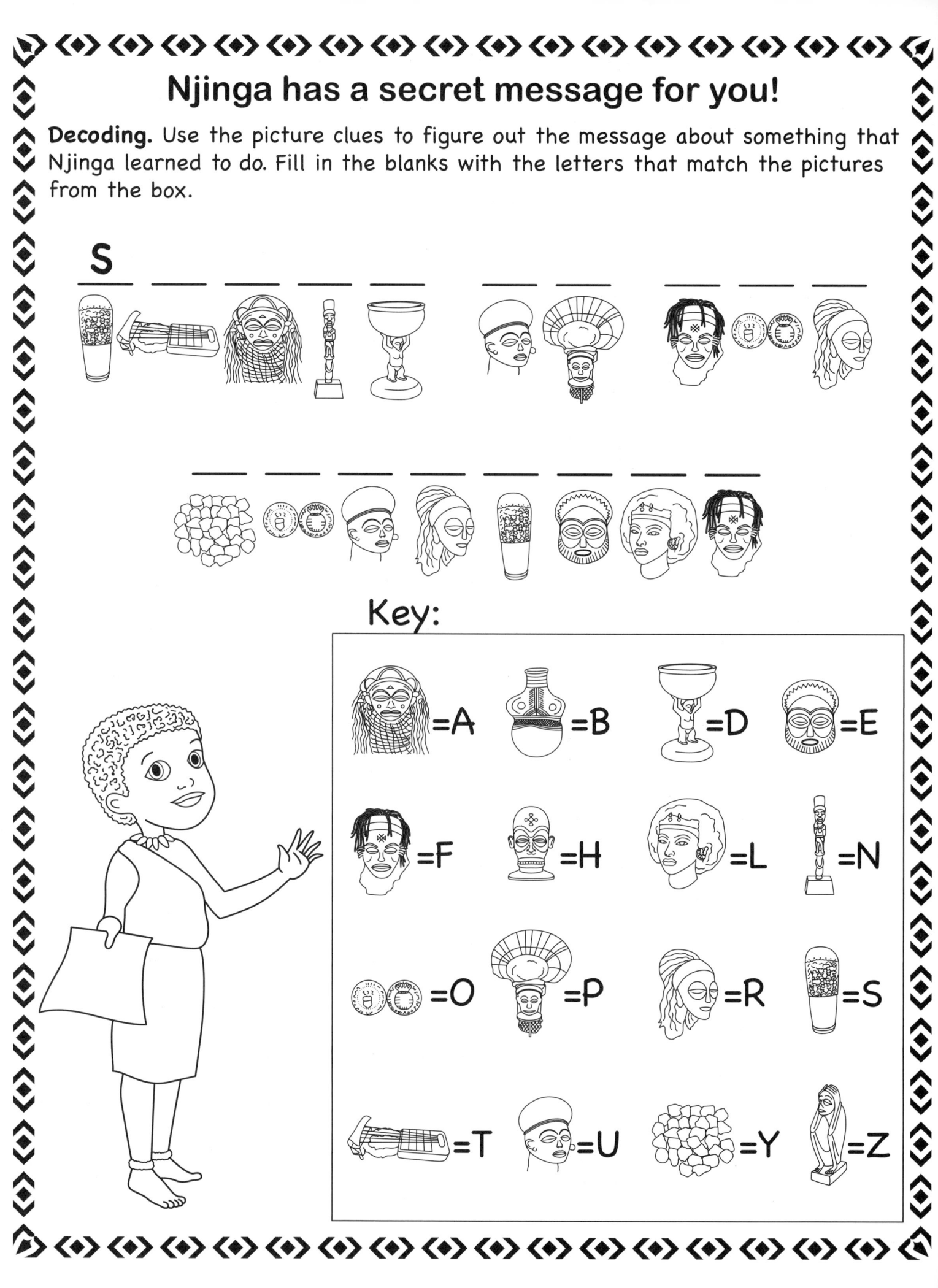

All about Njinga's Life

Crossword Puzzle. Solve the crossword puzzle about Njinga's life.

Use these words from the story: Njinga, Soba, Mbandi, Ngola, Mukua-mbele, Matamba, brave, outsmart, talent, Ndongo

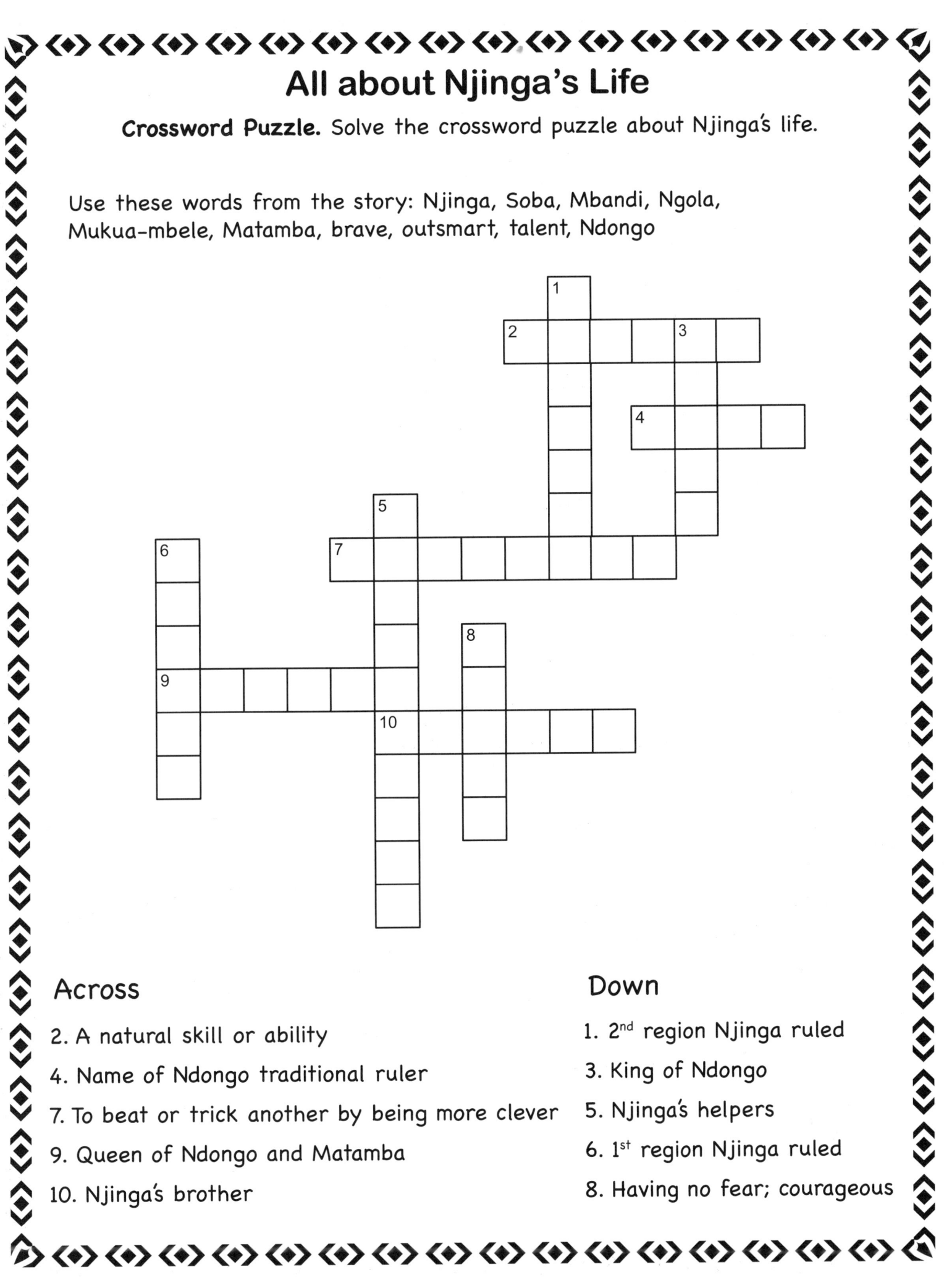

Across

2. A natural skill or ability
4. Name of Ndongo traditional ruler
7. To beat or trick another by being more clever
9. Queen of Ndongo and Matamba
10. Njinga's brother

Down

1. 2nd region Njinga ruled
3. King of Ndongo
5. Njinga's helpers
6. 1st region Njinga ruled
8. Having no fear; courageous

Solving Riddles

Letter Code. Can you figure out the answers to these riddles? Using the key at the bottom of this page, fill in the blank areas with the corresponding letter below each number.

1. I have a spine but really no bones. What am I? __ __ __ __
                                                                                          8 20 20 10

2. I am a group of fish and a place to learn so many things. What am I?
   __ __ __ __ __ __
   13 1 16 20 20 2

3. I can be small or big. You put me in order or say me out loud.
   __ __ __ __ __ __ __
   14 15 17 8 3 5 13

4. I am an African country. My name is "an adult female sheep" and "an adult male goose" combined. What am I?
   __ __ __ __ __ __
   15 6 4 14 12 4

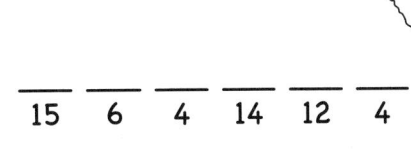

5. I come from a palm tree. I am brown and hairy on the outside, and white and creamy on the inside. Who am I?
   __ __ __ __ __ __ __
   1 20 1 20 14 15 7

6. I can come in handy when you need to measure something or command a kingdom. What am I?
   __ __ __ __ __
   5 15 2 3 5

7. If I'm not my sister or my brother, and we have the same mother, who am I?
   __ __ __ __ __ __
   17 9 13 3 2 18

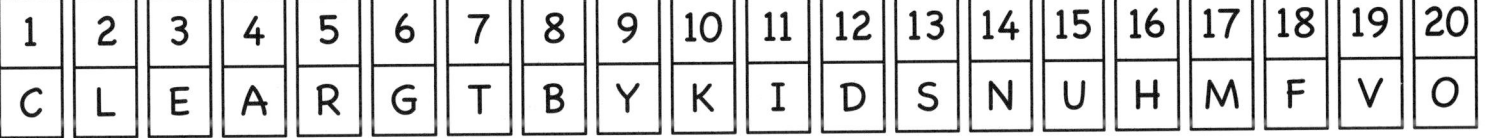

1	2	3	4	5	6	7	8	9	10	11	12	13	14	15	16	17	18	19	20
C	L	E	A	R	G	T	B	Y	K	I	D	S	N	U	H	M	F	V	O

Geography of Angola

Word Search (Provinces in Angola). Find the 18 provinces listed below in the puzzle. The answers are written across, down, diagonally, and backward.

Did you know? Angola is divided into 18 provinces. Luanda is its capital city.

Language Exploration

Let's Learn the Languages Njinga Spoke. Njinga showed us how well she could recite her numbers in Portuguese. Now it is your turn! Fill in the blanks with the Kimbundu, English, and Portuguese translations below.

Kimbundu ⟹
English ⟹
Portuguese ⟹

1
- moxi
- one
- um

2
- ladi
- ___
- ___

3
- ___
- three
- ___

4
- wana
- ___
- ___

5
- ___
- five
- ___

6
- ___
- ___
- seis

7
- ___
- seven
- ___

8
- ___
- ___
- oito

9
- divua
- ___
- ___

10
- ___
- ten
- ___

	1	2	3	4	5	6	7	8	9	10
Portuguese	um	dois	três	quatro	cinco	seis	sete	oito	nove	dez
Kimbundu	moxi	ladi	tatu	wana	tanó	samanó	sambwadi	dinak	divua	dikuinhi

Ancient Languages

The Kimbundu Language. Match the Kimbundu words used in the story.

Soba	School
Ngola	Twist
Pangueami	Tired
Xikola	Helpers
Njinga	Traditional Ruler
Kuhoka	King
Mukua-Mbele	Brother

Your Talents

Self-Expression. Everyone has a talent. Talent is a natural skill of ability. Njinga shared a talent for leadership like her father. Draw a picture sharing your talent. Write about it.

My Talent

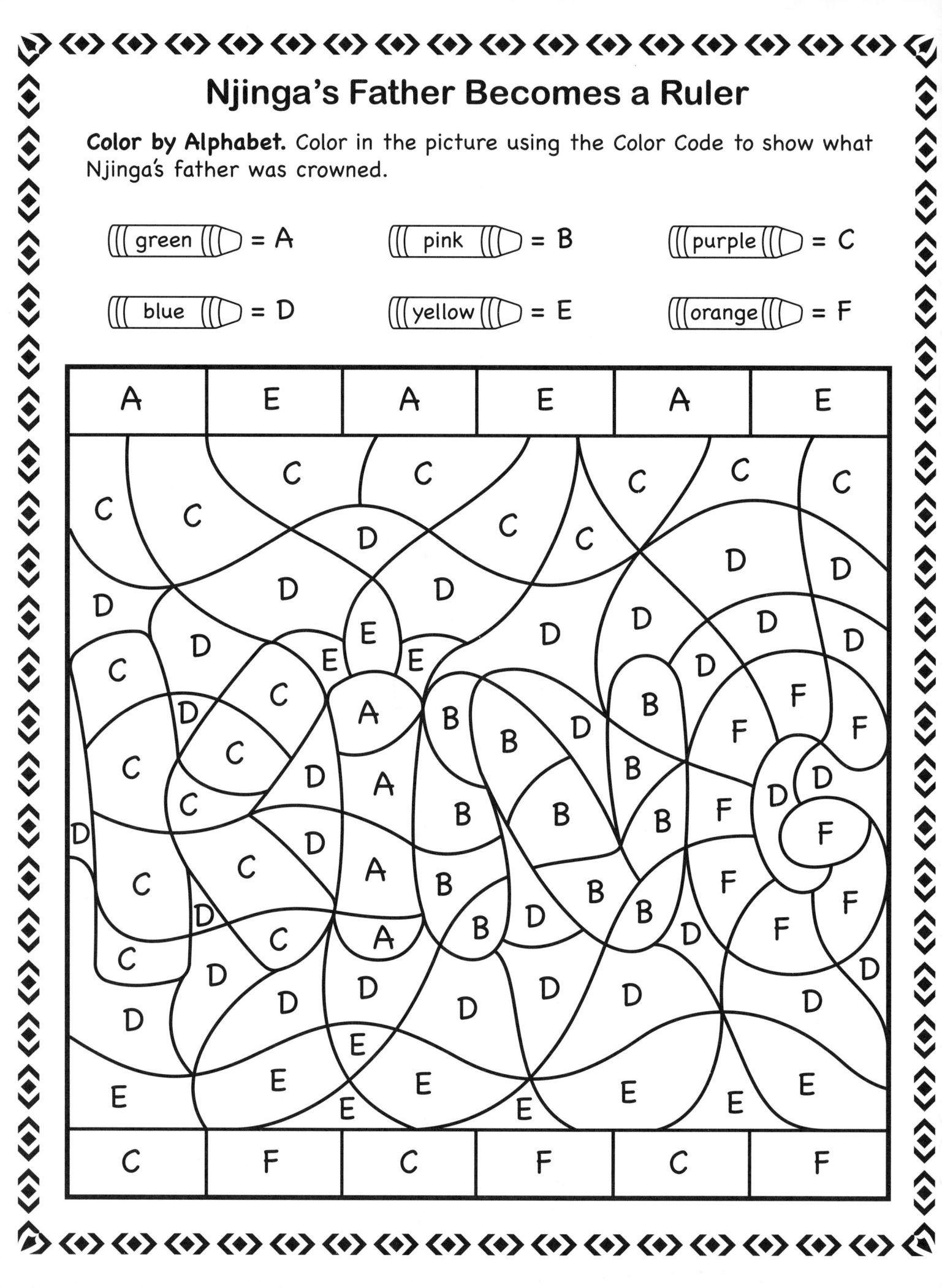

Njinga is teaching me!

Self-Reflection. Put a checkmark in the boxes to show what Njinga wants you to learn.

- [ ] To be brave
    - [ ] To listen in class
- [ ] To be disrespectful
    - [ ] To stand up for myself
- [ ] To fight for what I believe in
    - [ ] To gossip
- [ ] To be responsible
    - [ ] To care for others
- [ ] To hurt my brothers and sisters

Journaling

Creative Expression. Write a journal entry about how Njinga felt when her father passed away and she chose to flee the kingdom. Add a title. Use 3-5 sentences. Draw a picture of her escaping.

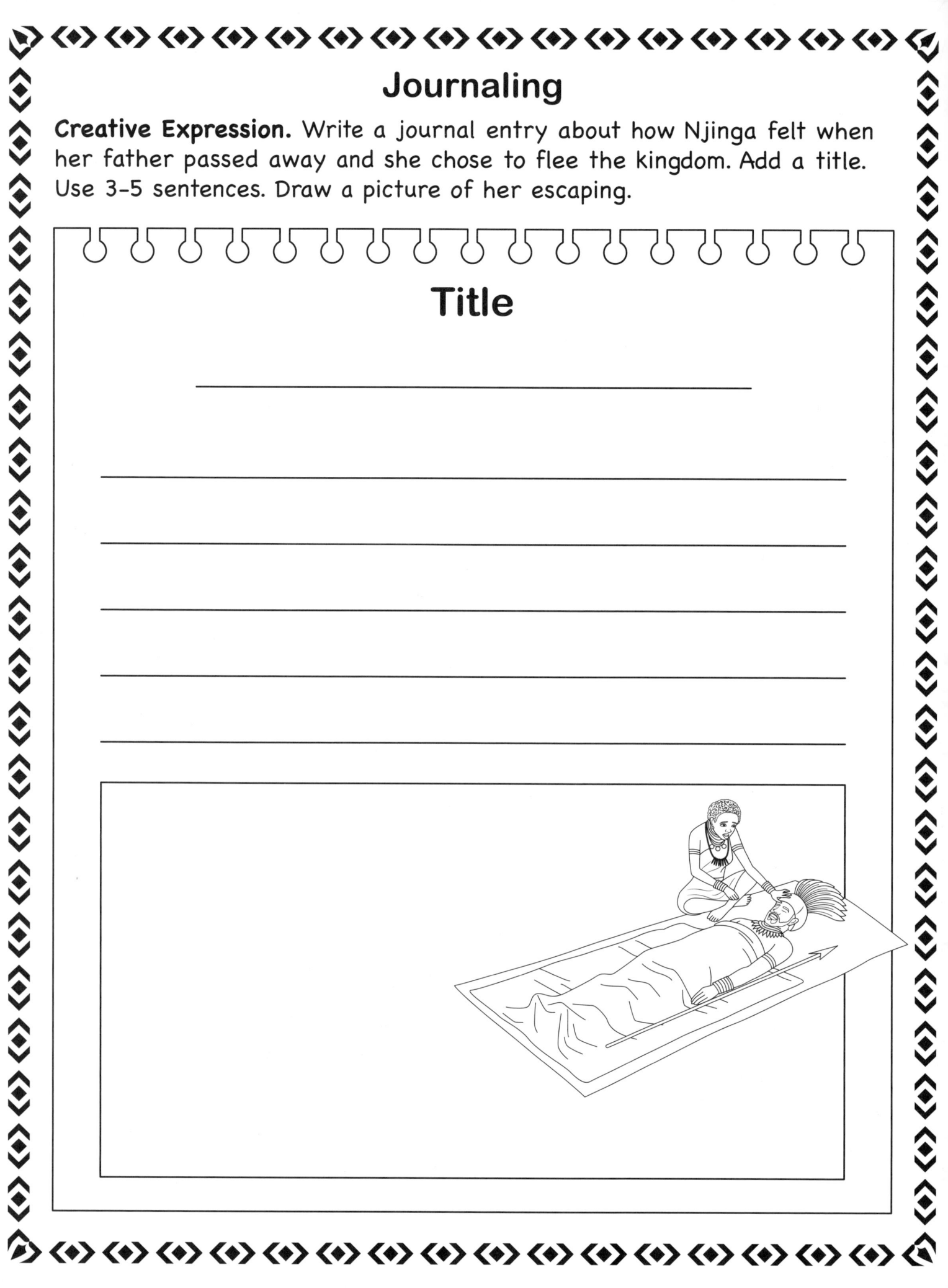

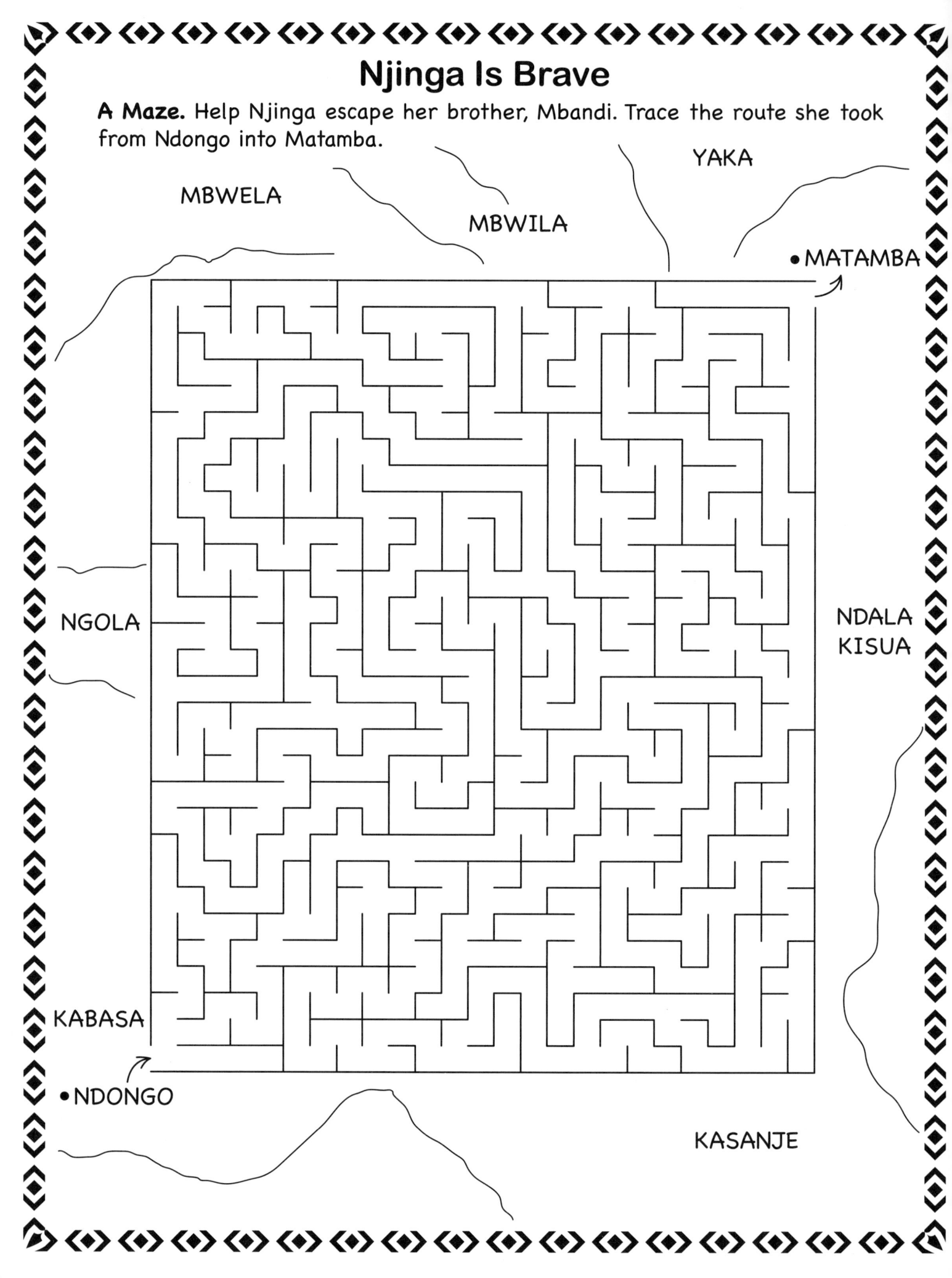

Guess Who?

All About the Characters. Which of these phrases best describe the characters in the story? Draw lines from the phrases to the characters. All characters have 2 answers.

1. Father

2. Njinga

3. Mbandi

a. named for the word "twist"

b. was jealous of Nzinga

c. taught business and battle tactics

d. wasn't treated as an equal by the governor

e. firstborn son

f. breathed air into daughter to live

Improving Your Outlook

Self-Reflection Activity. Njinga teaches you to be strong in mind and in ability. To achieve the things you want, you need the right mindset. Think about the behaviors below. How often do you do them? Then pick at least one or two behaviors, and write a plan about how you will improve this behavior.

Growth Mindset Checklist Affirmations

Growth Mindset Behavior	Always	Often	Not Yet	My Plan to Improve
I learn from my mistakes.				
I pay attention in school.				
I am brave.				
I say what I believe.				
I don't allow anybody to bully me.				
I care for my loved ones.				
I do not give up.				

Board Game FUN!

Getting to Know Africa Board Game (for 2-4 Players). You will need one copy of the board game, a pair of dice, and a token for each player. Players take turns rolling the dice to go around the board to get to the finish line. The first player who gets to the finish line wins!

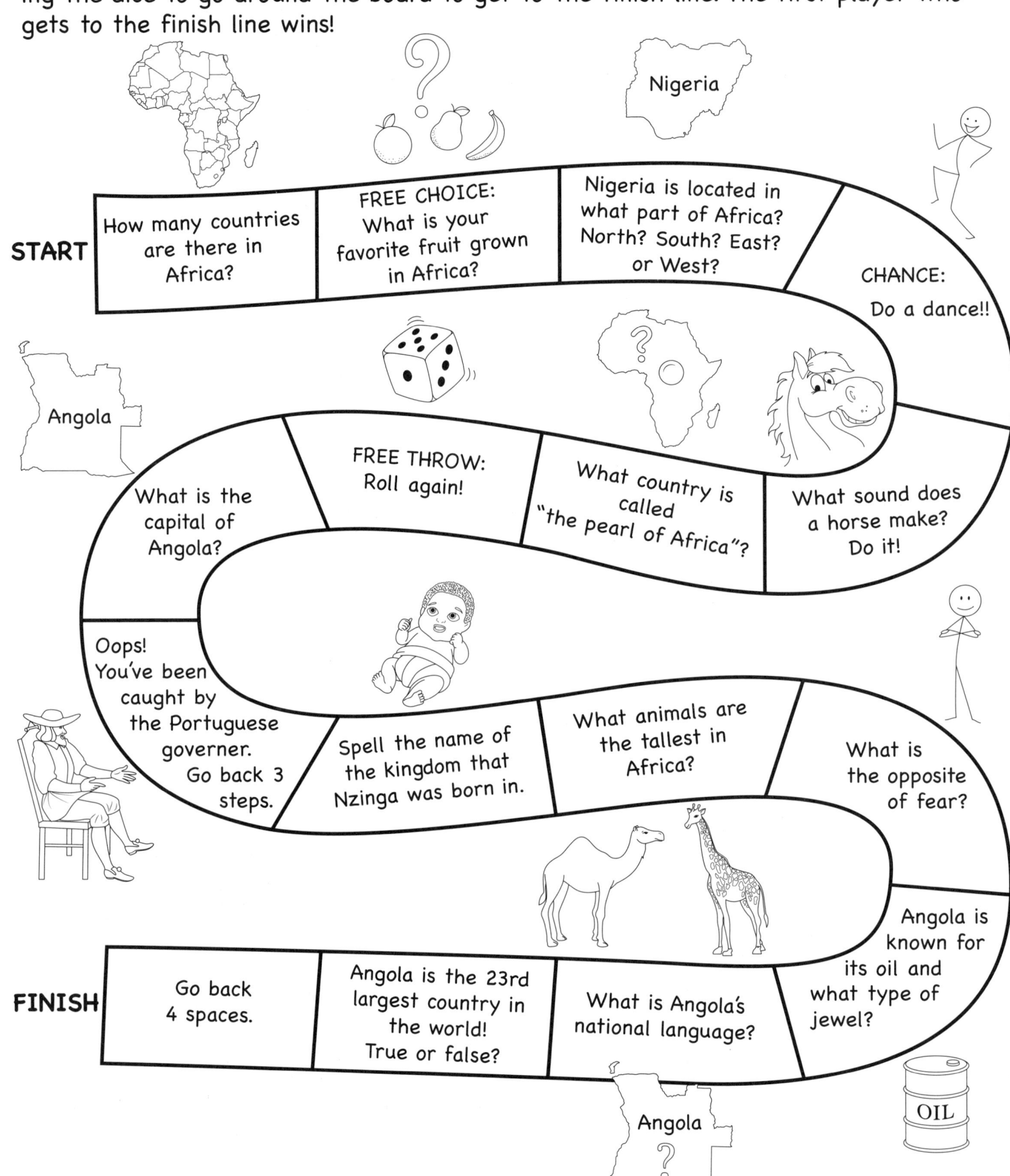

Njinga the Warrior

Dot-to-Dots. Connect the dots to help Njinga run away to Matamba.

Understanding the Story

Multiple Choice. Circle the correct answer to each question about the story.

1. What evidence in the story suggests that Njinga was clever?
    a. She was younger than her brother.
    b. She quickly learned how to recite her numbers in Portuguese.
    c. Her father loved her very much.
    d. Her father breathed air into her so she could live.

2. What evidence in the story suggests that Mbandi was jealous?
    a. He had many friends at school.
    b. He did not want Njinga to go to school.
    c. He asked his sister to come back and help him rule.
    d. The Portuguese took over, and demanded riches and slaves.

3. What is most likely not a reason that Njinga's father became king?
    a. He protected the people.
    b. The people admired him.
    c. He was skilled as a fighter and in business.
    d. He was a tall man.

4. What do we know about the Portuguese governor, Dom João Correia de Sousa?
    a. He could speak many languages.
    b. He was a ruler for a long time.
    c. He did not always treat Njinga as an equal.
    d. He had several brothers and sisters.

5. What is most likely the reason that Njinga could be queen of two kingdoms?
    a. She liked to travel.
    b. She could speak several languages.
    c. She was confident, clever, courageous, and determined.
    d. She was the younger sister of Mbandi.

Story Elements

Answer the Questions. Use complete sentences to answer these questions about the story.

1. Why was the nurse frightened at the beginning of the story?

_____

_____

2. How did Njinga get her name?

_____

_____

3. What reason did her father have for sending Njinga to school?

_____

_____

4. Describe 2 things that her father did to train Njinga as a future leader.

_____

_____

5. What happened to the Kingdom of Ndongo when Mbandi became a ruler?

_____

_____

6. Why did Njinga leave Ndongo when her father passed away?

_____

_____

7. Why do you think the Portuguese governor listened to Njinga?

_____

_____

8. Explain how Njinga became queen of two kingdoms.

_____

_____

Getting to Know the Author

Author's View. Think about the author of the book. Then answer these questions in complete sentences.

1. Why was the story written?

_____

_____

2. Explain the importance of the picture of Njinga sitting on her helper's back when she spoke to the Portuguese governor.

_____

_____

3. Do you feel that women and men can both be good rulers? Why or why not?

_____

_____

Art Exploration

Looking at the Illustrations. Look at the pictures in the book "Njinga of Ndongo and Matamba." Draw your favorite picture.

What Came First?

Help Tell the Story. Number the events from the story in order (1-12) of how they happened. The first one is done for you.

(   ) Njinga's father passes away.

(   ) Njinga convinces the Portuguese to leave Ndongo.

(1) Njinga is born.

(   ) Njinga goes to school.

(   ) Njinga's father takes Nzinga to attend business, and she learns about war.

(   ) Njinga is forced to run for her life with her helpers.

(   ) Ngola Mbandi loses control of Ndongo, and Njinga becomes the queen.

(   ) Mbandi sends word to Njinga that he needs help as a ruler.

(   ) Njinga travels to speak to the Portuguese governor in Luanda.

(   ) The story of Njinga's birth spreads throughout the land.

(   ) Ngola Njinga conquers the Kingdom of Matamba and moves her people there.

(   ) The Portuguese government takes over Ndongo, then demands riches and slaves.

Angolan Mask

Dot-to-Dots. Connect the dots to draw a wooden mask carved from the Angolan people.

My Mask

Drawing: Angolan Art. Can you draw your own Angolan mask?

Did you know?

- The Chokwe of Angola use this beautiful mask called Mwana pwo in their initiation ceremonies. The mask is used to remember female ancestors.

- Mwana Pwo means "young woman."

- The masks are said to bring fertility, peace, wealth, and well-being.

Getting to Know Angola

Fill in the Blanks. Write the missing words to discuss Angola.

Use these words: Kwanza, red, Botswana, gold, Ngola, dreadlock, black, gold, 1975, Portuguese, imbondeiro, black, Atlantic Ocean, Kimbundu, Namibia, Brazilian samba, Zambia, red, Tchokwe, Democratic Republic of the Congo.

- The country of Angola gets its name from the Bantu Kingdom of Ndongo. Their name for the king is ....

- .... is the main language spoken in Angola. Other spoken languages are Umbundu, ..., Kikongo, and ....

- Angola gained independence from Portugal on November 11, ...

- The local money is called the Angolan ....

- The Angolan flag is ...., ..., and .... The .... part of the flag stands for the blood of the people who were killed in wars; the .... stands for the Angolan people; and the .... stands for the industry and the peasants. The star on the flag of the former Soviet Union.

- Angola is bordered by the .... to the north and east, ... to the east, and .... and .... to the south. It also has a coastline along the .... to the west.

- .... dance is thought to have begun in Angola where it's known as "semba."

- Angola's national tree is the beautiful ....

- Angola is the birthplace of the .... hairstyle.

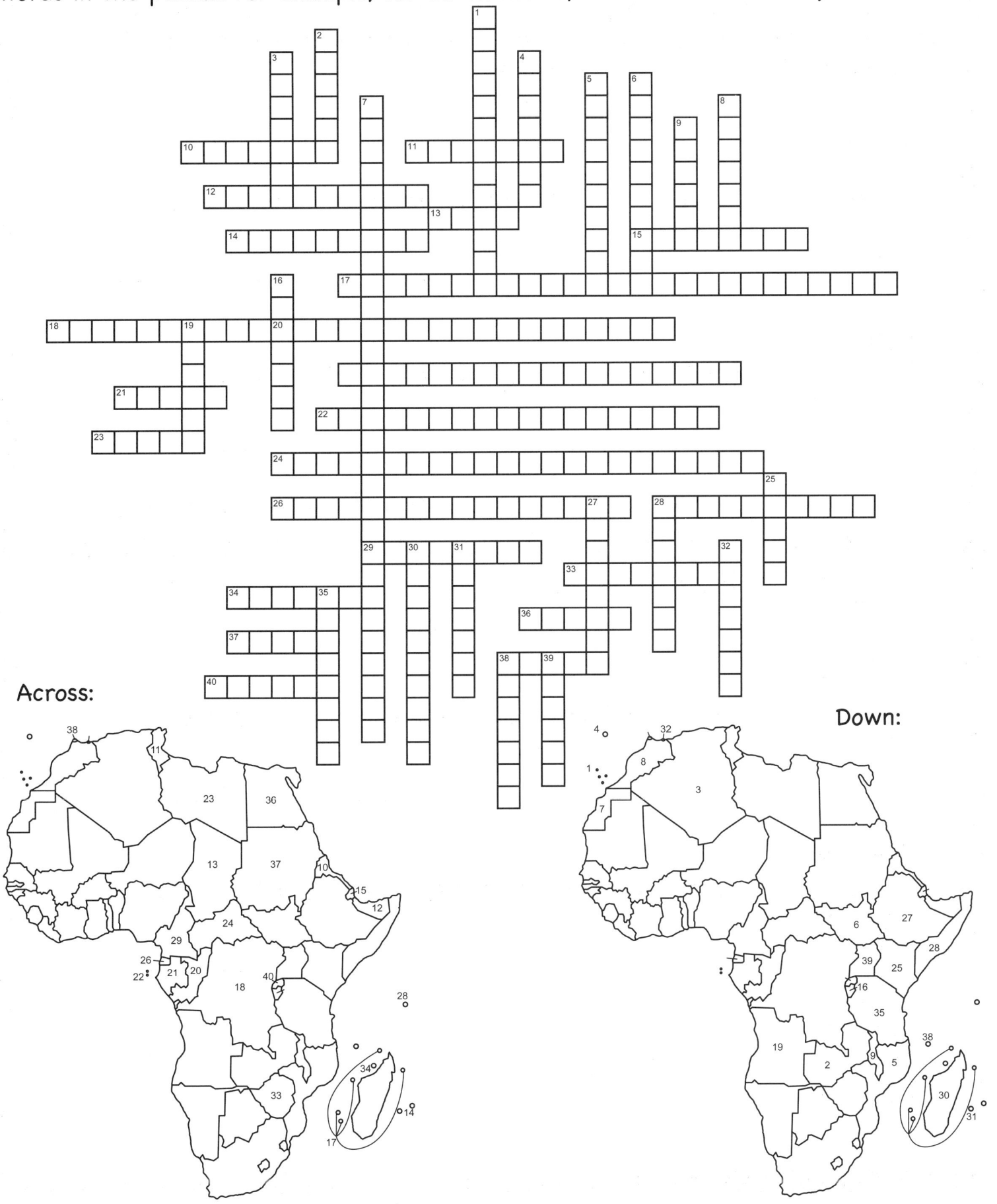

Getting to Know You

Njinga of Ndongo and Matamba Icebreaker Game (for 2-3 Players). Cut 6 slips of paper. Each slip of paper should have a number 1 through 6. Place the slips of paper into a cup. Players take turns pulling out a number from the cup. They answer the question to the group.

⚀ What is something new you'd like to learn?
_____

⚁ What do you hope to be when you grow up?
_____

⚂ Njinga's name means "twist." What does your name mean? If you don't know, what would you like it to mean?
_____

⚃ Explain when you were jealous of someone.
_____

⚄ Name something interesting about Africa.
_____

⚅ What can you do when someone is rude to you?

ANSWER KEY

All About Njinga's Life - Crossword Puzzle
Across: 2. talent, 4. Soba, 7. outsmart, 9. Njinga, 10. Mbandi
Down: 1. Matamba, 3. Ngola, 5. Mukua-mbele, 6. Ndongo, 8. brave

Solving Riddles - Letter Code
1. Book, 2. School, 3. Numbers, 4. Uganda (EWE + Gander), 5. Coconut, 6. Ruler, 7. Myself

Geography of Angola - Word Search

Ancient Languages - the Kimbundu Language
1. Soba - Traditional Ruler
2. Ngola - King
3. Pangueami - Brother
4. Xikola - School
5. Njinga - Twist
6. Kuhoka - Tired
7. Mukua-Mbele - Helpers

Guess Who - All About the Characters
1. c, f,   2. a, d,   3. b, e

Understanding the Story - Multiple Choice
1. B,   2. B,   3. D,   4. C,   5. C

ANSWER KEY

Story Elements - Answer the Questions

1. The nurse was frightened because baby Njinga had had a difficult birth and was not breathing.
2. Njinga's name comes from the word "twist" because her mother's umbilical cord happened to be tied around her neck at her birth.
3. Njinga's father sent her to school because he could tell that she was smart.
4. Njinga's father prepared her to be a future leader by sending her to school, and inviting her to attend meetings and battles with him.
5. When Mbandi became ruler, the Portuguese started demanding more slaves and riches from the people of Ndongo.
6. Njinga left Ndongo when her father passed away because she knew that her brother had always resented her. Because of this, she was worried that he might harm her.
7. The Portuguese governor listened to Njinga because she spoke Portuguese, she was confident, and she was diplomatic.
8. Njinga became queen of the Ndongo kingdom when her brother (who was king) disappeared. As queen of Ndongo, she faced many battles and threats. She conquered the kingdom of Matamba to provide more safety for her people.

Getting to Know Angola - Fill in the Blanks

- The country of Angola gets its name from the Bantu Kingdom of Ndongo. Their name for the king is Ngola.
- Portuguese is the main language spoken in Angola. Other spoken languages are Umbundu, Kimbundu, Kikongo, and Tchokwe.
- Angola gained independence from Portugal on November 11, 1975.
- The local money is called the Angolan Kwanza.
- The Angolan flag is red, black, and gold. - The red part of the flag stands for the blood of the people who were killed in wars; the black stands for the Angolan people; and the gold stands for industry and the peasants. The star on the flag is of the former Soviet Union.
- Angola is bordered by the Democratic Republic of the Congo to the north and east, Zambia to the east, and Botswana and Namibia to the south. It also has a coastline along the Atlantic Ocean to the west.
- Brazilian samba dance is thought to have begun in Angola where it's known as "semba."
- Angola's national tree is the beautiful imbondeiro.
- Angola is the birthplace of the dreadlock hairstyle.

Don't Get Puzzled - Central and East African Crossword

Across: 10. Eritrea, 11. Tunisia, 12. Somaliland, 13. Chad, 14. Mauritius, 15. Djibouti, 17. French Southern Territories, 18. Democratic Republic of the Congo, 20. Republic of the Congo, 21. Gabon, 22. São Tomé and Príncipe, 23. Libya, 24. Central African Republic, 26. Equatorial Guinea, 28. Seychelles, 29. Cameroon, 33. Zimbabwe, 34. Mayotte, 36. Egypt, 37. Sudan, 38. Ceuta, 40. Rwanda

Down: 1. Canary Islands, 2. Zambia, 3. Algeria, 4. Madeira, 5. Mozambique, 6. South Sudan, 7. Sahrawi Arab Democratic Republic, 8. Morocco, 9. Malawi, 16. Burundi, 19. Angola, 25. Kenya, 27. Ethiopia, 28. Somalia, 30. Madagascar, 31. Reunion, 32. Melilla, 35. Tanzania 38. Comoros, 39. Uganda

This activity book accompanies our "Njinga of Ndongo and Matamba" picture book.

Head over to www.our-ancestories.com to grab your copy.

Our Ancestories
www.our-ancestories.com
contact@our-ancestories.com

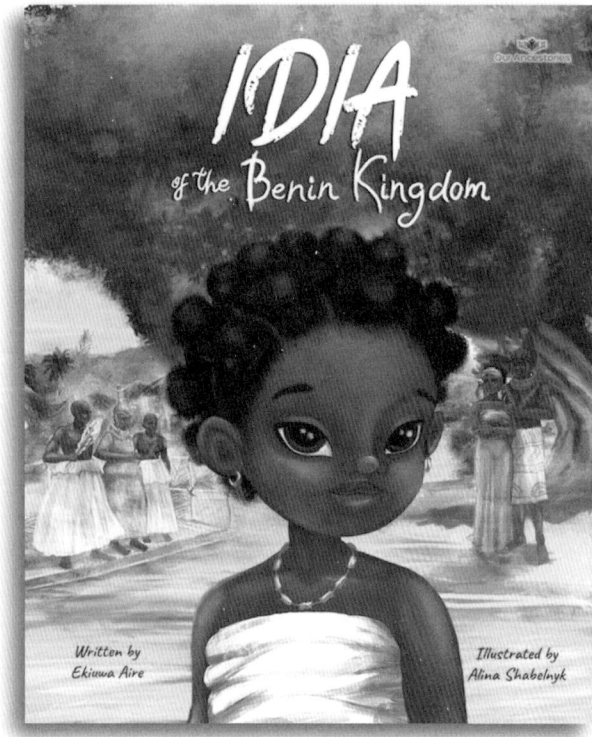
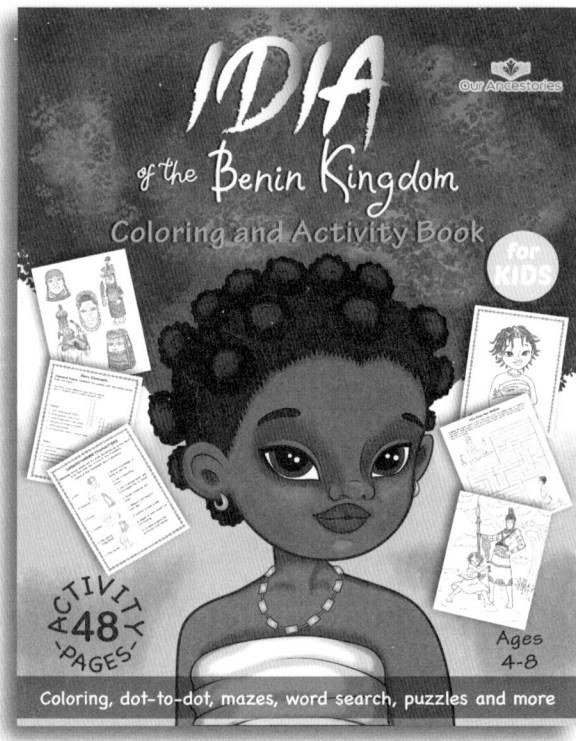

Get the entire collection, comprehensive teacher guides and more at
www.our-ancestories.com